Katya Romanoff

A Dozen Deepest Wishes

Illustrator
Anna Zakashansky-Zverev

Translated from Russian
By **Svetlana Mitchell**

c.

Order this book online at www.trafford.com
or email orders@trafford.com

Most Trafford titles are also available at major online book retailers.

Translated from Russian by Svetlana Mitchell
Illustrator Anna Zakashansky-Zverev

Printed in the United States of America.

ISBN: 978-1-4669-8960-3 (sc)
978-1-4669-8961-0 (e)

Library of Congress Control Number: 2013907486

Trafford rev. 07/10/2013

 www.trafford.com

North America & international
toll-free: 1 888 232 4444 (USA & Canada)
fax: 812 355 4082

Against the backdrop of summer's green
The dandelions, those fuzzy parachutes
Are busy paving secret trails
To the four corners of the earth.
These fair-haired postmen
Carry wishes in tiny little envelopes,
Up there, in heaven, each wish expected
And for each, believe it, there is a directive.
Here is where my deepest wish was plucked
And carried over the hillside
'Tho I sent it long ago, I am still waiting
For my verdict, I've yet no reply.
Such is a wish, a deceptive thing,
It'll slip away, by chance, and off, off it flies,
And a wish of ill-will may turn into torment
Should it be granted by the skies.
And dandelions soar up toward the light
Only to disappear in the alcoves of the universe,
And still they keep flying, a sign of summer
And that all wishes will surely come true.

***

And so, one Dandelion on duty
Was visiting the neighboring estates,
In a dashing belted kaftan,
Inherited from his parents.
His was a special assignment
From the post office "upstairs"
To fly around all the flowers nearby
And find out what they wish for.
What's on their mind, what they dream of –
Write it all down and deliver the notes.
This task will take up some time:
Distances between the dwellings are long.

The Dandelion hurried to begin his duty,
First stop: the Rose, the object of his secret admiration –
After all, she is one that visits us in dreams –
Flew into the garden, and here is what he sees:

Rose

In the morning glory of a summer garden
The divine Rose lazily yawns,
Seemingly bored, but happy deep inside,
Enjoying this dose of drowsiness.
At least for one day, in the silence and coolness,
To give a bit of rest to the mortal body,
Refuse makeup, cancel all business –
"Arrivederci," she sang to it all.
Always surrounded by loyal admirers
How gorgeous is this queen of flowers!
She is the "winner" of pompous parades
And a queen of fairy-tale dreams.
Recordings, shootings, concerts, tours –
Life fractured into million pieces,
Must have enough time to play new roles
Before her final, swan song.
She must always be the most desirable,
"The one" for the millions,
Need time to lick the wounds
And keep sparkling, without breaking the canons.
Bright Rose, as if approachable:
It seems you can touch it and pick it by hand,
But she keeps on the defensive,
Concealing sharp thorns in thick foliage.
Amid the bustle of her admirers,
And her popularity that can be cruel –
It has been written by poets –
She is brilliant, yet … lonely.
This diva has been looking for love through the years,
Throwing herself into the deep end every time;
It's well known: there is no fashion for feelings,
Yet again, the Rose resigns herself to suffering.

Our Dandelion was a bit shy
To approach the beautiful Rose,
But he asked her, in spite of his fear,
To declare her wish out loud.
For a while, in deep thought sat the Rose
As the coffee was turning cold in the cup,
Even forgetting to change her pose,
While Dandelion was patient and quiet.
Her glance glistened through thick eyelashes,
The diva finally condescended:
"God! There is a limit to my patience!
I shall write it all down, not sparing pages!"
She swayed in great excitement
Exclaiming: "Thirst for love!"
"Tell me, is that a crime to lose yourself
And share happiness with the one you love?!
Do I not have the right
To ask for the blessing of love,
In place of my glory, to love and be loved,
Like any other flower?!"
Well, Dandelion acknowledged her wish,
Put away the intricate message,
Kissed Rose's hand in appreciation,
And flew away, with an easy smile.

Cactus

The garden where beautiful Rose daydreamed
Lay near an estate – quite enormous, in fact.
Sounds of thunder could not penetrate it,
A computer stood there in the quietness.
Nonstop, at the computer
A prickly Cactus bristled his needles.
Day and night he stared longingly
At the dust-covered monitor,
Like that mouse from its hole.
The ubiquitous web
Has lured and sucked him in,
Falling into the Internet abyss,
There is not enough sunlight for him.
Every day he looked for a remedy
From this global solitude,
Throwing himself into the net, looking for salvation
Among flowers without names.
He was sure of it: there lay his freedom,
He could be what he wanted to be,

It does not matter that there are no sunrises:
They can be forsaken for the time being.
Senses given from birth taken for granted,
The web with no flavors, no aromas
Swallowed him whole –
Silly Cactus, what a waste.
Our hero became incurable
Resigning to the matrix syndrome,
As he hit the keys neurotically…
Well, keep lying to yourself if you like.
Connected to millions
The Cactus remained alone,
And convinced of the power of the web
He grew inertly, pale and lanky.

The Dandelion slipped deftly
Onto the monitor in front of the Cactus,
"Hello Cactus," he repeated,
But could not start the conversation.
Immersed in this virtual world of his
Cactus noticed little around him.
"Postman in a flesh – such a banality,"
He must have thought to himself and stayed quiet.
Our Dandelion did not want to give up,
Determined to resolve the thorny issue,
He was going to see this through to the end,
And sent out an electronic request.
To his honest surprise,
He received a prompt reply.
This dispelled his old doubts:
The Internet could be handy in urgent matters.
In his brief and bold message
The Cactus simply stated
That he was ready to confess.
His words were screaming in the letter:
"I wish to be always successful!
For starters, at least on the net.
I promise to make a diligent effort,
As long as I find my happiness!
Maybe somewhere beyond the fragile screen
There is a soul similar to mine
That is zealously looking for me,
Somebody lonely and nice!"

Dandelion printed out the letter,
And replenished his mailbag.
He most certainly knew: magic won't happen;
There is no other way to the skies.

Orchid

He has already set foot on the threshold
Prepared to leave the welcoming abode,
But he wasn't able to leave just yet
As he awed with amazement.
Basking in the golden rays of the sun
As if a statuette frozen in the window,
Orchid appeared right before him,
And drew him in, like Medea, the sorceress.
Her full, youthful lips
Framed the sensual mouth,
And her large, pearl-like teeth
Would bare for anyone who was not a miser.
Parties, hairstyles, dresses,
Shoes at the height of fashion,
And the varnish on top –
She wasn't yet old.

The Orchid, in her glamorous disguise,
Had one purpose only – to seduce.
She did not bother with propriety,
If the object was rich – can't stop her.
The evening trumpets invariably
Called the diva to new campaigns;
At all the prestigious night clubs
She was treated like a VIP.

She would set up her trap there
On a man with a fat wallet,
And keep her victim at gunpoint
Pretending to be innocent.
A dazzling Orchid
Wanted to live in the world of gloss.
"Here is an idea: get married!"
All that was missing was the right match.

Dandelion exhaled
And approached the stately diva.
She looked sternly from above
On his courteous bow.
"What do you want, Dandelion?" –
She uttered carelessly.

"I'm here strictly on business" –
Was his impassive reply.
He stated his business in detail:
Such and such, please share your wish,
So? – She skillfully lit up a cigarette,
And took up her letter with purpose.

You may have already guessed it:
The Orchid wished for money,
That was her dream – no fault of her own
When the Cote d'Azur beckons.
She kept writing clearly, with zeal:
"To you, Creator, I'm writing,
To tell you without hiding:
For me, happiness is
To live in Manhattan or Paris.

I want to dine in fancy restaurants,
Wash down calamari with wine,
Not ever fumble through my pockets,
And sleep soundly through the night.
I want to wear only diamonds
And clothes "*haute couture*,"
And be surrounded by dandies –
No right ones yet, although I've met a few.
In short, I need a rich man,
A husband ideally, of course,
For all the reasons above
I'm counting on a jackpot."

Our servant from heaven put away
The Orchid's message with all the others.
He wished her good luck, as was the ritual,
Slightly bowing in farewell.

Dahlia

Dandelion was anxious to continue
His journey ahead, which was still long,
Next, he decided to disturb
A Dahlia, sprawled out wide.

Dahlia was a family man,
A wonderful father to his many children.
If you only knew how many sweets
He has provided to everyone's delight!
Never lazy, a hard worker,
He made sure his children had plenty to eat.
All the worries and all the expenses
Were carried by him.

He was such a reliable fellow,
And a caring friend to many,
Maybe a little old fashioned,
But with family life full of grace.
As he grabbed his kids in his arms,
He laughed whole heartedly,
As if reliving his own childhood,
And the sons adored their Papa.
To teach them kindness – there's a task,
Dahlia set good examples.
With a gentle push from their father
Each son was growing up tenderhearted.

He surrounded his offspring with tenderness,
They were growing up full of blossom;
He made their lives fairy tale-like –
That's what they call "Salt of the Earth."

Dandelion landed swiftly
In the heart of the happy family,
And in great detail revealed
Why he was there.
He tried hard, and he was at his best
Unveiling his goals.

They took to liking him right away
Touched by his passionate appeal.
Raising his eyebrow, the father Dahlia
Strictly looked over his family:
"I won't hide it: there is more than one wish,
But I will tell you my most cherished:
Nothing is more important for me in the world
Than my children's good health,
And that later the kids of their own
Would become their support in life.
Let them turn into beautiful flowers
That spread joy all around.
As long as good deeds count
They will be happy."

Our messenger heartily accepted
The father's golden wisdom,
He nodded his fair head
In silent consent.

In a dexterous move, he picked up the note –
Served faithfully, no nonsense,
Firmly shook hands with the family,
Turned around – and off he went.

Carnation

He did not fly for too long
When Dandelion saw a Carnation.
It is impossible to miss her face,
She is not a needle in a haystack.
She stood confidently on her stem,
Tossing her short hair.
She could win in any fight – you could tell,
As tough as any street-smart, feisty fellow.

Businesswoman: no more, no less,
Serious, presentable lady,
She easily managed to get around on time,
No drama, cool headed.
Her day is planned out to a minute:
Agreements, meetings, auctions,
They are strung like beads on a string
On a woman's delicate shoulders.
There is no big surprise:
Carnation was a true feminist.
Born to be a career woman,
She couldn't stay in the shadows.
She truly believed, and rightfully so,
Her "sisters" were equal to men,
So she broadcast that loud and clear
Regardless of personal motives.
She had many admirers –
She was really attractive,
But with them around, like a bird in a cage,
Her soul was tormented.

She wanted to be audacious to the fullest:
He who is not on her side – out of sight.
Carnation, full of energy and strive:
Don't get in her way!

13

Deliberately polite, the Dandelion
Asked for permission to enter,
And because he was not a local,
The hostess was tempted.
"Did we have an appointment scheduled?" –
Icy tone, bypassing the propriety.
Poor chum, he looked very pitiful –
This job was getting harder by the hour.
"Hmm, okay, you have three minutes.
Tell me why you are here. Well?!
You look all funny with your cheeks inflated.
What are you mumbling there? I can't understand!"
The postman was slightly taken aback
By such a blunt approach,
But he didn't travel all this way for nothing,
The last thing he needed now was a quarrel!

Once again, with intentional courtesy,
He repeated his explanation,
Even though he lost his enthusiasm,
Carnation displayed some patience.
She suddenly paused for a moment,
Slyly narrowing her eyes,
And said in sudden resignation:
"I should be grateful to you.
I won't lie: I do have a wish.
I can achieve many things in life:
I'm cut from a different cloth,
And often ahead of the game.
I strive to reach the highest of heights
That the business world has to offer.
To be the leader of a corporation –
That would be a great honor!
To be the first one on the markets,
And make my way into the world,
My job is stressful – that is true,
But I'm prepared to pay the price!
Well, my dear, that'll do it!
Time for me to run…"
Dandelion uttered with dignity:
"I won't hold you up."
He sealed the envelope slowly,
As if to spite the hostess,
Checked the clock on the wall,
And ceremoniously left Carnation.

Burdock

He was about to fly up in the sky
When he heard a raspy bass:
"Hey bro, since I bumped into you on my way,
Treat me to a cigarette, just once."
"I'm sorry, but I don't smoke" –
Replied Dandelion to the talker, and
He looked closer and noticed
In the thicket the Burdock's land.

The slacker slumped free and easy,
Clinging to everybody who walked by,
A rollicking weed, the Burdock
Was glad to see a dimwit-newcomer.

Our Burdock was a rare bully;
With him around, the terrain turned to gullies.
Among neighbors, he was notoriously unruly,
After all, the fella could really drink.
He considered himself smarter than most,
Really thought the world revolved around him.
He was vulgar and obnoxious with others,
So nobody could stand him.
He had dropped out of school,
And never acquired a skill,
When there was work, he would slowly trudge.
The worthless Burdock lived an idle life.

And if once in a while
He earned a little money,
His days flowed by inertia:
Sitting at home and drinking away.
A burden to his own family,
Irresponsible, insolent beast,
Like a billiard ball rolling into a pocket,
He was headed toward chaos and waste.
Thus in drunken stupor and idleness
His youth has passed him by.
Even though we all meet our match,
Burdock's own wife has left him.

Right away Dandelion caught on
That he was trapped by the weed,
So he figured he'd tell him the news
Not to provoke this dangerous volcano.

When he heard the message from heaven,
Burdock roared: "That's it!
I will finally have a wonderful life,
Covered in chocolate, fairy-tale like!
So here's what I need: I want to meet
A duped flower who can't say "no" to me,
I would glue myself to it with all my might,
And be dependent on it for everything –
In terms of provisions and money.
I would swim in abundance,
And be spoiled with beer and honey,
And live for my own pleasure.
So tell me, Blondie,
Can you fulfill my wish?
Or I'll punch you in the face for sure,
You'll have to work hard for a cure!"
Here the Burdock chuckled triumphantly
And loosened his strong grip.

Dandelion looked very pale –
And he hurried to get out of there.
He backed away from the villain,
Whispered stuttering: "I'll d-d-do what I c-c-can."
Our postman wouldn't wish it on his enemy
To come face to face with Burdock, the hooligan.

Daisy

Dandelion soared toward freedom!
He won't soon forget this rendezvous…
Exhausted, he landed in a field,
To collect his thoughts and take a break.
He took a deep breath, recovered,
Scolded himself for this mistake,
And was ready to move ahead,
When standing in front of him –
Was a Daisy, a shy smile on her face,
A peasant's white kerchief on her head.
She looked at the world trustingly
Like an innocent girl from a picture,
Open to all the winds
That blow through the fields.
Modest and often overlooked,
Daisy has accepted her destiny.

She had a son and a daughter –
It so happened by accident.
A single mother, Daisy
Was desperately looking for happiness.
She lived a simple life,
Walked barefoot all her life,
Nourished by her rosy dreams
And by the grace of the sky above.
She worked hard from dawn 'till dusk,
Earning her bread and butter,
And if someone for help would ask,
Daisy was always there for others.

Lovers read their fortunes by daisies:
Loves me – loves me not –in my heart stays.
Yet Daisy herself does not know
Where her own beloved is.
This yellow-eyed beauty
Smiles for all – ear to ear,
After all, will anybody really care
That she is ready to die for love?

The Dandelion was parched,
So he asked for a drink from Daisy.
Always affable to all,
She offered him some water, clear and cold.
Our messenger regained his strength,
And shared with the hostess his path;
Daisy was ever so pleasant,
So he didn't mind making the moment last.
When asked about her deepest wish,
She blushed like a poppy, turning red,
As if she was revealing a deep secret
And taking a very important step.

"If only it were possible…
If only it could come true..." –
She began cautiously,
Which was a sign of sincere modesty.
"Hey, be brave," Dandelion encouraged:
"Believe me, in heaven, all are equal,
And all wishes are valued.
Trust me: I am a courier, not a crook."
Daisy rustled her dress:
"All right," she agreed,
"I really wish for happiness

Even for the tiniest critter.
May we always be merciful
And kind to one another.
Then happiness will certainly
Will find its way all around.
And all flowers – small and big –
Will rejoice and be happy.
Perhaps, I will not be forgotten,
And my Cornflower will finally find me?"

Though Daisy's words were naïve,
They also had indisputable reason.
Dandelion filled out his papers:
A customer's wish was a law.
Our postman warmly parted,
With the "yellow eyes" so welcoming,
And rushed away at full speed
Through the sunlit field.

Sunflower

Our courier was sailing through the field
As emerald as the deepest sea.
On his course heading forward
He caught a glimpse of a tall beacon.
Bright yellow, lean Sunflower
Propped the sky with the top of his head.
All around him the lively waves
Swelled and played tag.
Lifting his face right up to the sun
He relished in its golden rays.
In the zenith, he looked like he was
Cast out of bronze by a hand from above.

The Sunflower's calling was
Of an artist and a creator,
The picture was worth a thousand words –
God gave him talent for his effort.
In the entire neighborhood
He was truly one of a kind,
And in some mysterious ways
In the elite circle he stayed.
Sunflower's life was not refined,
His homestead unadorned.

He earned his living as a free worker,
And always held his head high.
He believed that one can live a life of the poor,
Yet be filled with inspiration.
To him, a lot of sun could do no harm,
In other words, he wasn't a typical creation.
So independent, this artist
Was quite happy in his solitude,
Only a light summer rain, uninvited,
Would visit His Majesty, the Sunflower.
Maybe he was not so lonely,
With his gang of apprentices
Who vowed to him
To do only good, and not evil.
Their heads, so clever and bright
Grew darker from day to day,
And they kept improving their craft
To be accepted by Mother-Earth one day.

At first, the postman landed nearby
And tried to strike a conversation,
But his efforts made no effect –
He needed to yell up high.
So he rose to a higher place,
Face to face with the artist,
Noting to himself that the Guru
Was marvelous, if a bit stern in the face.
Dandelion grunted with a strain:
"I'm a postman from heaven on a mission,
I've been ordered to collect wishes,
So I'd like one from you, dear friend."

Sunflower laughed out loud:
"I already have everything I need,
God has not forgotten me –
I've had countless conversations with Him.
To the Creator, I'm closer than most,
So what else could I possibly wish for?
Maybe only for the sun to keep
Shining upon the meadow?"
"Well, that sounds like a wish – great!"
The postman pronounced with care –
"Then I didn't pop in here in vain,
Keeping diligent in my job, to be fair."
Our Sunflower shrugged his shoulders:
"Very well, write down the message."
He had enough of the visitor's speeches,
So the Dandelion went on his way.

Daffodil

A thick grove appeared
At the edge of the wide field.
Looking for a cover from the heat,
The postman headed for the cool of the trees.
He lowered himself almost to the ground,
Enjoying the invigorating shade,
And inquired from the young grass
If there were any flowers around.

The grass rustled briskly:
"Who are you? Where are you from? From whom?
Although it is not important,
Go ahead and find the old brook.
There, you will find what you are looking for,
The flowers that live there are not common.
They are of unearthly beauty!" –
Little stems giggled in chorus.

Dandelion at once became antsy,
Intrigued by what lay ahead.
The grove stood still and sleepy,
As if under a magic spell.
In the low-lying land
The postman noticed the tranquil brook,
He followed it half way
Flying hastily right behind.

At last, he saw Him,
As slender as a cypress,
Swaying ever so gently,
The Daffodil in its lush plumage.
He stood at the edge of the stream
And admired his own reflection.
The water that flows belongs to no one –
He adores this situation.
Daffodil was hopelessly ill:
Blindly in love with himself.

Surely, anyone is free to love,
So this poser relished his freedom.
Always manicured
And impeccably groomed,
He loved being among glossy fools
Resembling him in appearance.
He was rather squeamish,
So he preferred cushy jobs,
It's not that he was all that lazy,
But he didn't break a sweat at work.
Elegant, selfish Daffodil,
Wasteful and a big spendthrift,
A bit of an artist, a bit of a buffoon,
Was keeping up with the breed.

The Dandelion dared to interrupt
This session of self-admiration,
So he called the Daffodil by name
To get his attention.
This was by no means easy –
With the other too fixed on his image,
Didn't have time to enjoy it in plenty –
Only the self-absorbed would understand it.
Nonetheless, on the fourth or fifth attempt
The Dandelion succeeded,
For poor Daffodil, this was such a torment
To deny him these sweet delights.
He was extremely outraged,
His eyes sparkling with wrath.
Our courier said his quiet prayers
For this indignation to pass.
He started blabbering, tedious and incoherent
About the purpose of his visit,
But as if doing him a favor,
The Daffodil simply smiled.

Finally, the poser gave his answer:
"I want to live a high life,
I have no secrets about it,
I'll say it out loud since you asked.
I want to have trendy clothes,
Designer labels – not something lame,
And above all, have all the hot girls
Go crazy about me.
Let's be honest, I'm a handsome devil,
And a giant, in a sense.

Oh, and a bag full of cash, while we are at it,
Then, come on, play it up – that'll be grand!"
And on this "high" note
Dandelion waived his goodbye;
He has already heard somewhere
A very similar desire.

Tulip

The postman continued further
Along the winding creek,
The twisty, dodging, supple trees
Made way for him.
At the top of a light colored hill
Where the creek bubbled like a fountain,
In the forest's spacious backyard
Stood a marvelous Tulip, like a sentinel.
He stood at attention sturdily,
As only soldiers can,
And watched the surroundings closely,
Until the sundown.
The Tulip dearly loved the open spaces
Where he was born and grew up,
For all who relied on him for support
Responsibly he served.
The entire neighborhood had no fear
As long as the Tulip was near.
And their biggest pain
Was facing hail or rain.

He was a brave young fellow,
Saving those who were defenseless,
Throwing himself fearlessly into a battle,
In his cape of red-hot petals.
And even when Tulip was weaker
Than the bully-opponent,
He rushed forward with all his might,
Paying with his blood in the fight.
He was attentive and partial
To concerns of other flowers,
And from the locals he always had
A warm welcome and a roof over his head.
All the young girls sighed over him
And secretly followed behind.

They probably even dreamed
Of being protected by him from harm.
For the righteous cause – steady as a rock,
Always honest to himself,
Fighting misfortune and evil,
The Tulip was an everyday hero.

When he noticed the postman
The Tulip asked if he needed help.
The other replied: "Yes, I really do,"
Eager to start their discourse.
He was happy beyond words that they have met,
And wanted to make a good impression,
But the evening snuck up on them,
So with that, he slapped his pockets,
And went right down to business
Without further ado.

The Tulip was quite surprised
How friendly this courier was.
He was deep in thought for a while:
Have taken the question to heart.
Dandelion listened carefully
Writing down everything that was said.
It was clear, the Tulip was modest
Wanting nothing for himself,
Yet the wish turned out enormous,
On behalf of many others he asked for help.
He spoke: "I want justice
In resolving various matters;
To have a little more truthfulness,
And have a limit to rudeness.

We should all be tolerant toward one another,
And denounce all violence,
And not think we deserve a pat on the back
For these righteous efforts.
Every flower should be valued,
And all have equal rights,
And if you are mean or lazy,
Be accountable for your own actions."
Dandelion adjusted his kaftan,
And once again filled his mailbag,
Remembered that it was time to hit the road,
And left the Tulip so heroic.

Immortelle

The postman could feel the weight of his load,
But he was pleased with what he has collected.
He decided that it wouldn't be too much of a trouble
To get two or three more letters.
A dove-colored evening lay on the threshold,
And the darkness kept creeping in,
And that's when on the hillside
He saw another lonely flower.
He flew up as close as he could,
And stared at the creature.

"This flower cannot be real" –
Our postman was not in the know.
It seemed there were no signs of life:
Petals – dried out scales –
As if radiated light,
But nature has a different glow!
Dandelion was ready to be on his way –
What was the point in staying?
The flower suddenly opened its mouth: "Hey,
I think it is my duty to help you."
"Excuse me, but what is your name?"
Babbled our postman,
The flower cried out at once: "Immortelle!"
"My time has finally come!"

You could say that the Immortelle
Held a public service position.
He was a clerk, in appearance and in mentality;
His relations were not based on friendship.
Keeping busy all day long,
He appeared unapproachable,
So that all sorts of "nobodies"
Didn't bother him with their nonsense – have they no shame?
Yet, if somebody important
Stopped by for a visit,
He would get off his high horse,
And showed respect and honor.
He made a lot of promises,
And could really talk the talk!
Evidently, he was not afraid of God,
To be littering with words so publicly.
When it came down to actions,
He would hide in the bushes, and not a peep.
Yet he diligently sent his reports up the ladder,
As in "we are plugging away, in spite of the enemy!"

Our friend Immortelle was two-faced:
Called himself "a servant of the people;"
In reality, he was a freeloader,
Mooching off this "rabble."
He enjoyed a decent salary
For shuffling papers from pile to pile,
Had no scruples with filling his own pockets,
A true bureaucrat, in short.

The Dandelion hid his embarrassment,
And explained who he was and why there.
The Immortelle started to schmooze
As soon as he heard the good news.
He exclaimed: "Without fail!
This very instance,
I will state my wish with precision,
And detail it all at once."
The Immortelle turned to the letter
With eagerness, as if it was a report.
Clearly, for him it was a familiar matter,
And even something he was proud of.

The Dandelion tried to stay patient
As the bureaucrat's pen kept squeaking,
The letter flowed as long as the Volga,
And so did the cool of the night…
Without a doubt, the greedy Immortelle,
Tried to squeeze in more than one wish,
"Ah, office-rat, bureaucrat! Damn you!" –
The postman was ready to wail.
So what did this diligent scribe want?
Quite simple – he wanted longevity,
Many more things – the paper will endure it all –
His wishes and interjections:
"Ah! I wish for as long as possible
To remain in my current post,
I could always use more authority,
So I would like to get more seniority.
I want to keep eating as sweet,
Sleep as tight, and be well received everywhere,
To not ever lose any privileges,
And to always please my superiors…"
On and on the letter went in the same sentiment.
Should we really keep reading it?
What else was left for our courier to do –
But to make haste with the letter in hand?

Lilac

The Dandelion suddenly realized
That time has come to finish his task.
He carefully checked all the envelopes,
Making sure not a single letter was lost.
By now the night was pitch black.
The overstuffed bag over his shoulder
He slid down the narrow footpath
Leading up beyond the forest.
He did not yet get up too high
When he heard someone whisper:
"Dandelion, please stay a while,
I promise not to grumble.
I won't take much of your time,
I know that it won't be easy for you
To make the long journey back home
In the dark by yourself."

Our postman could not ignore
This speech, so unusual,
He had nothing to argue with,
So he allowed it to slowly flow.
Perched on a roundabout fence,
He bashfully greeted Lilac,
He was charmed and disturbed at once
By her magic.

She continued talking slowly,
Her speech flowing like honey,
And her simple, powerful words
Kept on ringing and soaring:
"I know you are gathering wishes,
And you have made a great impression,
And will hand deliver upstairs
A multitude of deepest confessions.
I, too, have decided to state
What moves me deep inside,
I can no longer torment my soul,
And my wish is great.
I have lived in this world a long time,
Having gathered all the wisdom I could,
I've kept to myself this wisdom of mine
Until this prophetic hour.

Time has come to share with others
What I know and what I value,
And to you, postman, this knowledge
I will now promptly reveal.
Don't lose heart or give into boredom
Even when the skies are grey,
The rain will end, and so will your torment,
A rainbow will appear and make it all go away.
Send out only positive thoughts,
So that your body doesn't shiver,
If those thoughts brightly burn
In the sky, as if giant bonfires.

Wish for peace for yourself and for all:
Each one of us is fragile,
Treat everybody with respect,
Words, too, can have a painful effect.
Because if you pluck even one blade of grass
On one end of the world,
On the opposite end, the entire Universe
May shake like glass.
To sum up what I want to convey,
Here is my wish:
That our world could not be destroyed,
No wars – they ought to be banned!
So that no one has to know
This evil tragedy ever again.
Let us live and love from hence forth
And raise our children and gardens!"

Those were Lilac's measured words;
Listened trustingly Dandelion.
But their watches had been synched,
So they said expeditious goodbyes.

The postman just about fulfilled his mission,
Having visited all the flowers,
The only thing left was to deliver
The letters to their final destination.
All those deepest wishes
Added up to exactly a dozen,
Dandelion was flying overloaded
But happy: his trials were over!
Swiftly balancing on his stem,
He headed skyward over the sleepy grove,
Ran up the moonlit path
And … disappeared into the night.

Will the flowers' wishes come true?
Who knows? We shall wait and see.
Only it seems to me, that we must first send
Our good intentions to the sky.
A wish is like a bird in hand –
Can't catch it once you let it fly.
First think hard, remember they say:
"Measure twice before making a cut."
Often, a wish is in no hurry to come true,
Whether you get angry or not,
So you need to make an effort yourself
To make each dream a reality.

Dandelions soar into the heavens,
Faithful messengers of the universe,
Not by accident miracles happen,
After all: my wishes do come true!

Printed in the United States
by Baker & Taylor Publisher Services